SAVVY
SELF-PUBLISHING

for the
Savvy Self-publisher

Zachary Black

ISBN-10: 1502412144
ISBN-13: 978-1502412140

Publishers:
Paperback: Zachary Black / Createspace

DEDICATION

To you, the self-publisher, may your creative juices bubble and boil and the words you crave keep flowing. I hope your chosen vocation lives up to all your expectations.

DISCLAIMER

I am not an authority on this matter. The information I share is part subjective, part factual having self-published and researched the subject at hand. The aggregators I discuss are all good, reputable companies and all offer a good, professional service. The information I provide is accurate at time of publishing.

This book is a print version of my website, compiled to demonstrate the print-on-demand process. The contents of this book and even more useful information, links and tools can be found for free at...

www.savvy-selfpublishing.com

If you wish to purchase a physical copy, the small royalty that I earn will go to...

www.cancerresearchuk.org

Thankyou

CONTENTS

ACKNOWLEDGMENTS

I would like to thank…

Nats for being pure granite.
Ben, I hope you enjoyed your noodles.
All those who make self-publishing possible.

INTRODUCTION

I want you to consider the information that I set before you food for thought, pointers to get you on the right track and help you make an informed choice according to your requirements, to help get you self-published. It is not an in-depth analysis of self-publishing.

Let us assume you have written a book. You think it's great, and your friends and family tell you it is. Now brace yourself... Have you ever considered they could be killing you with kindness? If you are writing because you share a passion for the art, great, keep going, indulge your imagination. If, however, it is your desired vocation, and you hope to earn a crust, before you invest your savings, I urge you to read on. It could save you more money than you're likely to make from self-publishing.

Success

How do we measure and define success? My ambition was to write a novel. I did, and I now consider myself a success. I have five star reviews on both Amazon and iBook store, and I am also fortunate to have recouped my investment and have made a modest profit.

The majority of self-publishers will have invested hundreds of pounds, sometimes more, keen to have their book in circulation. A few are lucky to have broken even, but not many. Why? They did not do their research, nor their sums. The process of self-publishing can prove to be somewhat overwhelming. Before diving in feet first, do your homework, at least have a basic comprehension of how the self-publishing machine serves its clients.

A number of years have passed since I self-published my first novel. It was frustrating. I had no idea what aggregator would best serve me, and my mind boggled as I researched conflicting articles and self-publishing guides. If only I knew then what I know now. Hindsight is a wonderful thing.

I am not going to drone on about how to write a book, nor, am I going to give a lesson in literacy, I am not qualified. I will leave that to the professionals. What I aim to do is give you a checklist, a brief understanding of the process and keep you from wasting your savings on those who make a fortune out of aspiring authors. I hope to share what I have learnt along the way so you can make an informed choice and publish your work confidently.

LET'S MINGLE

It is no easy task, writing a book. The very fact that you have managed to keep your bum planted firmly on the seat and have written a hundred or so pages is an achievement in itself. Be it drivel or a masterpiece you deserve at the very least congratulating.

It is one thing having completed a book; the hardest, most-frustrating part is bagging yourself a publisher. A few do, most do not. And so the dejected ponder their future as 'wannabe' authors and fall by the wayside, their ego in tatters. The unwavering pick themselves up, dust themselves off and plough on, determined to fulfil their dream. And why not!

Before computers occupied a place in every home and the internet was at our fingertips giving access to untold resources and service providers, our fate was in the hands of agents who determined whether or not our work was worthy.

Finally, the internet has given us a lifeline and the great publishing powerhouses can no longer keep us in the dark. We have risen against our oppressors.

The eBook revolution has momentum, and we can now mingle with the chosen few. Now the public, not the publishing powerhouses, decide our future.

But this privilege can, if not careful, come at a cost. There are those who seek to profit from our ambitions. Aggregators are the closest thing we have to an agent, without them our work would only amount to PDF's floating around the web and self-publishing would be almost impossible. It is they who provide the services and tools that are necessary and are without doubt the fixers who get the job done.

There are numerous aggregators within the marketplace that cater to the needs of you and I. And let us not forget, they are a business, a business striving to make a profit. And they do.

Beware The Vanity Publisher!

Be under no illusion, when a company charges you to publish your work, they are a 'Vanity Publisher.' Most will take your money and leave you wallowing in a puddle of disappointment. Of course, they will produce your book, but it will remain in a state of limbo, neglected, marketing and sales will be negligible.

Authors who are fortunate enough to have been signed by a publishing company do not pay to have their work published and can enjoy the spoils i.e. an advance fee, which come with being attached to these mighty corporations. But, without a doubt, marketing is their biggest asset. It is this is what we the self-publisher envy most. For it is the publishing companies who drive the marketing campaigns, flex their media muscle and in return, take most of the profits for their efforts. Unfortunately, we the self-publisher do not have such clout. But, we do take most of the royalties and we also retain control of our work.

GET ORGANISED

If you are serious about your writing and want others to take you so, then you need independent feedback. You need someone who will offer express their honest opinion, be emotionally detached, and will not tell you what you want to hear. You need constructive criticism.

You are going to need a professional. A fully qualified editorial agent could prove costly, however if ever I was going to invest money in my writing, they would be top of my list. But there is another option, maybe you know an academic studying BA in English or Literature. If not, find one, it could save you a fortune and might benefit their course material or even their CV.

Whatever you decide, you are going to have to consider the following before having your work considered for appraisal.

The Manuscript

It needs to be of the highest standard, the best you can get it. Even if you have been lucky enough to find an academic to help you out, conduct yourself as if you were dealing with a professional editorial agent. Be respectful, consider they might already have a full workload, especially if they are still studying, or they will soon abandon you. If you are paying someone to give it a work-over, do not think you can submit a heart hearted effort. If you want to be taken seriously then act accordingly, don't burn your bridges, you want to publish another book, right?

If it is fiction you write, your story needs structure. Plot has to be tightly woven. You have to set up your character(s), make them believable, justify their motivations and have their goal clear and purposeful. Conflict is essential in driving your story forward before it is ultimately brought to a climax and then finally all the issues within your story must be resolved. Even when writing non-fiction, your work still has to have structure, facts must be accurate and researched thoroughly.

Do not settle on the first draft. As they say, writing is re-writing. It can take up to several drafts, maybe more before you have ironed out all the creases and plugged all the holes.

If writing fiction, 'Save the Cat' (I use the software version, which I have on both my MacBook Pro and iPhone, and they sync too! Or you can buy the book) is a great method for structuring and developing your story. I use it at the beginning of my process, and I always go back to it after completing a draft. If it is not for you, there are plenty of other writing utilities available to help improve your writing.

Synopsis

A synopsis paints the narrative development of your story, highlights plot, theme, characterisation and setting. It is the narrative summary of your book so remember to maintain the same narrative style of writing in keeping with your story.

It needs to be emotive, written in the third person applying past tense using he or she. Also remember to introduce your protagonist and other supporting characters and the obstacles and conflicts that motivate them. You only have a few short paragraphs in which to convey your story. The reader needs to know the world in which your character(s) thrive, which character(s) they will pledge their allegiance and spur on to the end, the stakes they face and the consequences if they fail to succeed.

A synopsis, be it factual or non-fiction, is your pitch, a detailed summary of your book, which sells if crafted correctly. Do not confuse this with the back cover summary. The synopsis is what you present to a Literary Agent, Publisher and, or Editorial Agent before submitting your book for appraisal.

Interior Formatting

Before you upload your manuscript, you are going to have to format your book. Most aggregators supply various templates to download, depending on the book size you wish to publish. Be under no illusion, it is going to be time-consuming. This game is not for the feint hearted. But that is a job for the Academic or Editorial Agent I hear you say. That depends on what service you employ them to do. And it is worth noting, different aggregators demand different specifications.

When my editor emailed the finished version of my manuscript, it was laid out correctly. However, a problem occurred when I copied it over to a template that I later downloaded. And to make it even more frustrating, the original document and template were both word docs. For some unapparent reason it threw everything out, spacing, justification, there were all sorts of issues, and it proved time consuming to fix.

To avoid this, before you even begin writing your novel, I would advise you decide on the aggregator you are going to publish with, download their print book template and work from that. That way, the finished edited version that you receive back from your editor should be ready to go.

If you cannot decide on an aggregator, then I would use the MS Word templates provided by Createspace. They have two types for every trim size, a 'Basic' and a 'Formatted' version. I would use the formatted version, which includes 'Author, Copyright, Table of Contents' etc. Do not worry about these yet. Concentrate on crafting your piece until it is polished and complete.

All eReaders require the 'Table of Contents' to be formatted to enable navigation when using an eBook. If you are using Microsoft Word, there are numerous walk-through tutorials available on the internet, YouTube, for example, covering this topic. However, most aggregators include this as part of their service.

Title

It needs to be catchy, easy to remember, thought-provoking AND search engine friendly. It is paramount if you want people to buy your book. When someone inputs your title into a search engine, you want it to appear on the first page of results. Put a lot of thought and consideration into this.

Summary

When shopping for a new book to read, potential buyers are drawn by the visual and the thought provoking, namely the front cover and the title. These two key elements are what lure them in and have them pick up a paperback or click on the link of an eBook for closer inspection. The next thing they do is turn it over to read the summary. It is worth noting that eBooks have the summary hosted on the same page with the cover.

It is the third key element that if crafted well, should hopefully bag you a sale. To achieve this, you need to stir up a hunger and leave them wanting. Remember the synopsis? Now you need to write the back cover summary. Revisit your synopsis and read it over, this may help you. Your title, cover and back cover summary combined should grab your target audience and hopefully have them invest in your book. First impressions count.

The back cover summary is an essential tool if you are to sell and market your book. You have to convey your entire book in a few paragraphs. There are lots of websites with advice on how to do this. Try reading the back cover summaries of other books. The method 'Who,' 'What,' 'Where,' 'When' and 'Why' is another useful technique that might help get you started.

WHO is your main character?

WHAT is the story? What does he or she want?

WHERE does this takes place?

WHEN does this take place?

WHY are your character(s) in this situation? Explain their motive.

It is common, having finished your book, to hate your work. If you do find yourself in a state of loathing, do not worry, it is a natural response. Put it away for a few weeks and take a break. Maybe start plotting your next novel until you feel you are ready to go back and read it again. Maybe it needs another rewrite?

Once you are satisfied, having read it through, jot down all the events that come to mind. You will usually find the that key events you have remembered are the main beats. Do you remember having seen a great movie, and you have to tell your friends about it? That is the summary. Remember not to give away the plot and subplots. You would not tell that to your friends would you? Would you!

Copyright

This topic has most people sweating under the collar. UK law automatically accredits copyright to your work if you are the original creator and not writing for an employer i.e. a magazine or tabloid. The law may vary depending on what part of the world you live.

It is important to protect your work as best you can. It is a simple process, so why not? After all, you have invested time and money in the development of your book. Use other books as reference and see how they include their copyright page.

A Professional eye

Now that you are ready to take the next step. Presentation, grammar and spelling, have to be masterfully crafted, polished until perfect and worthy of your customers hard earned cash. I know how eager one can be to get a book into the marketplace. But do not rush this, take your time. Customer reviews can sink or sell a product. They are your best friend or your worst enemy. A scathing review can undo all of your hard work in an instant. Reviews are probably the best and only form of marketing you have for your product. You need a professional eye.

APPRAISAL

If you are serious about your work, and I imagine you are, then I suggest your next step would be to employ the services of an Academic or Editorial Agent as I mentioned earlier. They will constructively scrutinise your work and go through it with a fine-tooth comb. You will be amazed how many errors and holes they flag up. Do not be alarmed, you have just spent weeks, maybe months on your project, your brain will be numb, and your eyes desensitised.

Scour your 'Friends' list on Facebook, maybe you have a buddy at the University of Oxford. If not, turn to the services of a search engine, type 'Editorial Agents' and sift through a myriad of listings until one catches your eye. I had considered numerous companies offering the so called editorial service, including the aggregators' in-house services, but they seemed too corporate for my liking and the service they offered felt somewhat clinical. I desired a more personal relationship, bespoke mentoring and, lucky for me, that is exactly what I got.

First an introduction by way of email, which seems

the norm now. They will then request you email the synopsis, including title and the first three chapters of your manuscript for their consideration. Shortly after, they will respond stating whether or not they wish to invest their time in your work. If they do, then they will request you forward the complete manuscript for their appraisal.

The following gives an insight into the levels of services an editorial agents will offer.

Proofreading

Spelling, punctuation and grammar.

Copy Editing

All the above plus polishing language.

Development Editing

All the above plus incorporating language editing with development guidance.

Book Critique

An assessment of marketability and development potential.

Author mentoring

Bespoke one-to-one support.

Ghost writing

Writing or rewriting.

Some of the above services are more involved than others; hence, different rates will apply. Budget will dictate what you can and can not afford. If you do throw money at your project, this is where I would recommend you invest.

Let us assume you have made a decision on the service that best suits you and your work. You have followed through with the introduction, emailed the first three chapters along with your synopsis and now you wait with baited breath for a reply. A week or so later, you 'log-on' and check your email. Your heart skips a beat, and you see a response. Let us take a positive slant... The Editor has requested that you to forward your manuscript. And you do. And you wait... and wait. Each day that passes feels like a week until, one day you check your inbox and hey presto, they have delivered.

Having read the manuscript, you notice there are a few things that you liked the way they were. No problem, you email the Editor, bounce the manuscript back and forth a few times until you are both happy, and you have the finished article. You are buzzing with excitement, but what now? Everything seems to grind to a halt. You want your novel published yesterday, but how do you go about it and with whom do you publish? Not so fast.

GET SAVVY

Cover

The majority of aggregators offer an in-house design service, with their team of designers. Save your money.

If you have an aptitude for art and design, are a dab hand at Photoshop and have the spare time, try the 'Build Cover' option or download a 'Cover Template' from your chosen aggregator and have a go.

I considered this, but I wanted my cover to look professional and did not have the time. I had to focus on my writing as I was still liaising with my editor, bouncing the manuscript back and forth. It is important to realise your weaknesses and constraints. Editing your work and designing your cover might seem like a great idea, but are you familiar with Photoshop or similar software to get the job done? Do you have the time to learn such software? Is your book a personal or professional project (If it personal and is going to be a present, then I would definitely take the 'Build Cover' route)? Do you have aptitude and time to do it?

If not, you are going to have to turn to someone that has. Graphic Designers, like Academics and Editorial Agents, are worth their weight in gold. IF, you find the right people. Both services are key to having a professional finished product at its best. It is a wiser investment than throwing your money at vanity publishers.

My partner suggested a friend of hers to design my cover. Matt Niblock (mattniblock.com), a mild-mannered graphic designer with over eleven years of experience and very handy at web design too! Like all professionals, he wanted to know my expectations and asked if I had an idea of how I wanted the cover to look.

I am a great believer in giving creative people the freedom to work their magic. I emailed over my manuscript, and he read it in its entirety to get a feel for the story before knuckling down to work and apply his creative license. Not all designers will have the time or patience to read your book.

I had delayed the process somewhat, having not been prepared and still I had not yet decided on an aggregator. As a result, I was not able to provide him with the cover dimensions required so he could upload the cover file. Another argument for deciding on who to publish with before diving in head first. If you do find it all too overwhelming, at least you can point your designer to the aggregator's website, and they can check it out for themselves.

e-Cover

Most aggregators have software that allow you to

build a cover free of charge. If you do decide to build an eCover, a 'Build Cover' option will be made available once you have signed up with your chosen aggregator. If you have already designed a cover or have had someone do it for you, it is simply a matter of having to upload the file before publishing.

P.O.D. Cover

If you do decide to go paperback, most aggregators have the option to generate a P.O.D (Print-on Demand) 'Cover Template' that you can download, once you have input 'Interior Type,' 'Trim Size,' 'Page Count' and 'Paper Colour.'

You will need to consider additional artwork for the spine and also the rear cover. The rear cover is to accommodate both the summary and place-holder. The barcode, a rectangular white box, is positioned inside the place-holder and usually sits bottom right.

You will need to supply your designer with dimensions for the 'spine width.' Some aggregators provide a calculator on their website to work this out. For the overall cover, you will need to know front and rear dimensions, spine width and bleed.

If you do decide to have a go at building a cover, BookBaby, Createspace and Lulu offer a free, user-friendly, 'Build Cover' option with a variety of styles once you have signed up, perfect for simple projects and the not so techie self-publisher.

Aggregator

Broadly speaking an aggregator takes a product from you, the seller, and redistributes it at a profit.

Some aggregators also sell directly to the public. Assuming you wish to distribute your work as an eBook, simply upload your manuscript to your chosen aggregator. They will then convert it to one of a number of formats in order to meet the requirements of their distributors i.e. Amazon, Barnes and Noble, iBook store.

It can be tempting to use more than one aggregator. If you do, or decide to at a later date, it would be wise to consider the different formatting requirements of each. To avoid complications, keep your manuscript simple. Save versions in 'folders' on your computer and label them accordingly.

The manner in which aggregators conduct their business varies. Some take a percentage of the sale of your product, whilst a few charge a one off fee and then an annual fee to continue using their service or possibly both. Aggregators have become very business savvy when it come to servicing the needs of self-publishers and offer a number of tailored services, some I've already mentioned.

Conversion

If you are not submitting your book as an ePUB, your manuscript has to be converted into a readable format so that it is compatible with the numerous eReaders that are available on the market today, iPad, Kindle, Kobo, Nook, are but a few that come to mind.

Conversion can prove to be frustrating, tedious and time-consuming if your technical aptitude is somewhat limited. Leave it to the professionals. Most, if not all aggregators convert manuscripts as part of their service, providing you can submit your manuscript as per their requirements. Usually doc, doc(x), html, pdf and rtf suit most.

Pricing

We all want what we think our book is worth. After all we've been hooked up to our computer by an umbilical chord for months, scouring our imagination, thinning the skin on our fingers down to the bone. The truth is we do not have the publishing powerhouses behind us bombarding the public with marketing strategies until they yield and turnout their pockets.

Let us assume, you have a title that rocks, a book cover worthy of the 'Turner Prize' and a synopsis that has the reader wanting like an 'alkie' in Iran. Why on earth would they spend £9.99 on an unknown author when they can buy a John Grisham at exactly the same price? Why would the public want to take a chance on us? They would not.

I am sure this has affected sales on my book dramatically. A lesson learned. My book went straight to the 'New and Noted' section on iTunes. It sat alongside the likes of P.D James, Peter James, Lee Child and Dean Koontz. If my pricing had been more reasonable, realistic, it would have generated more sales, sailed up the sales charts and held a respectable position, for a while longer at least. That is how you get your publicity.

My title was well placed, in the top ten percent. However, that is not where the money lies. You have to be in the top one percent if you hope to see the money and have people take you seriously. If you already have a book out there and you've realised the asking price isn't realistic, don't be afraid to drop it. I did, and it paid off. You never know it may gain momentum.

Promotion

It is wise to start promoting the release of your book before being released into the public domain. Tease and tantalise your potential audience, but whatever you do, do not harass them. It will seriously hack them off, and possibly get you a bad review. Think out your strategy and take the subtle approach. There are many ways to promote your book for free.

Twitter, Facebook, Pinterest, Instagram, LinkedIn, and YouTube are the obvious options and can be used to great affect if carefully thought out. After all, they are free! You could have a go at hosting a web page yourself, but this can take time and yet more money, especially if you are not tech-savvy.

If you do, remember to link to whoever distributes your book. You will need to know where to point potential customers if you want sales. Another reason you should know which aggregator you want to publish with before you begin the process.

You could also print business cards advertising your book, again remember to include links to relevant websites. Hand them out to people, leave them around in random places but remember, be subtle and considerate.

Publishing

The internet is awash with advice, reviews and blogs detailing the best way to go about self-publishing and which aggregators you should or should not pledge your allegiance to. There are some fantastic articles for you to read and digest. There are also some misleading ones.

I am going to list five major players competing in the self-publishing arena that I had shortlisted before committing to one. They are all worthy for your consideration, depending on your requirements. Choosing an aggregator boils down to personal preference. You have to evaluate and match the services they offer according to your demands and budget, of course.

BookBaby, Createspace (Amazon), KDP (Amazon), nook press (Barnes and Noble), Lulu and Smashwords.

Note, you will notice, two of the six mentioned belong to the Amazon brand; Createspace, who focus solely on P.O.D and KDP (Kindle Direct Publishing) who focus solely on eBooks.

eBook, P.O.D. or both ?

Of the six aggregators aforementioned (I'm treating Createspace and KDP as separate entities), KDP, nook press and Smashwords, do not offer a print on demand service and focus their business solely on eBooks.

Createspace and Lulu use a royalty calculator that allows you to realise your share of the profit once they have deducted manufacturing costs and of course, their share of the profits and base their fees on either retail distribution or wholesale manufacturing costs and have royalty calculators to serve both. Quotes are dependent on the book specifications you choose.

BookBaby operates a little differently. You configure your book specification, decide on any of the extra add-on options (in-house services), save a quote, sign up for an account, and then upload your files. Unfortunately, Bookbaby does not distribute print books, but they now offer e-commerce and webpage option at no cost to yourself, but do take 15% of your retail sales.

The very notion of having your work go to print and bulk ordering copies of your book to sell is most tempting. However, this will require investment of your cash so why bother for now? It is a massive outlay, and gamble, unless you have bulk pre-orders? The worst possible scenario is to have the floor space in your spare bedroom taken up with unwanted books.

Publishing houses monopolise the high street. Display windows and bookshelves are theirs to own. So, why shell out? Your goal is to make bank from your writing, not a loss. If you do decide to publish a paperback, go with a company that offers P.O.D, i.e., Amazon's 'Createspace.' They set an agreed royalty per sale, which is paid into a nominated account without you ever having to invest your money.

If you are set on publishing both an eBook and P.O.D. I would first publish P.O.D with Createspace, then having completed that process, select the option to 'Publish to Kindle' with KDP.

US Tax Treaty

If you intend to sell your books, eBooks within the United States and are a non-US citizen, it is important you declare your earnings with the IRS (Internal Revenue Service). For all non-US publishers, a 30% withholding tax is mandatory until you complete the required documentation and declare an exemption, which applies to a number of countries that have signed an agreed 'Tax-Treaty' with the US. The UK's rate of withholding currently stands at 0%. Other countries exemption rates will vary, dependent on their negotiated rate with the US.

The W-8BEN document is applicable to US publishers and also Non-US publishers that trade within the US who seek treaty benefits. Complete and submit this form to the IRS with the following information...

I.T.I.N. (Individual Tax Identification Number) for individuals.

OR...

E.I.N. (Employer Identification Number), if you are a business.

iTunes requires a publisher to download, complete and submit the W-8BEN before considering their book for the iTunes store. Nook Press and Smash Words will accept and sell you book, but retain the 30% withholding tax until a W-8BEN has been completed.

Createspace and Lulu requires you to log onto your account, complete an online form and provide your personal Tax ID allocated to you by the country with which you are resident. It is a much simpler process than going it alone and doing it via the IRS website. If, however, you are using Bookbaby as your aggregator, then relax, you have nothing to do, they deal with it their end.

You do have the option of focusing the sale of your book solely within the UK and EU and then do not have to concern yourself with the US Tax Treaty.

Instead of amazon.com, simply use amazon.co.uk to market and sell your books. Of course, it will limit sales via Amazon's 'Expanded Distribution Network', but as mentioned in a previous chapter, it is a service that did not make a difference to the sale of my book. You can always opt into both of the above services, if you so wish, at a later date.

Barcode

When designing the back cover for your printed book, your designer will have considered the 'Placeholder,' a white block, to be positioned on the bottom right-hand side and is approximately 26mm(H) x 36mm(W). It is for the ISBN Barcode to be added by whoever prints your cover. Some charge an extra fee to generate a barcode, some do not. You could utilise one of the free barcode generators available on the web and make your own. You can then download it in as a PNG or JPEG and email it to your designer to put on the 'Placeholder' they have already allocated.

If you decide to PUB-IT-YOURSELF and utilise a barcode generator, it is worth looking at other published works for comparison.

QR Code

A QR Code is a fast, reliable way direct customers to your products. It is an arrangement of square black modules in a square container, usually a square white background. It is read and interpreted by digital imaging devices i.e. a camera on a mobile phone.
First designed for the Japanese automobile

industry, it is now more widely used for marketing and PR because of its efficiency and ability to handle large amounts of data.

Metadata / Bibliographic Data

It is a collection of information relative to a specific book where metadata is organised into different categories. The ones most relevant to you when submitting your book for publication are…

ISBN
Title / Subtitle
Author
Publishing Date
Publisher
Price
Number of pages
Author's biography
Genres
Description (Short and Long versions)
Keywords

Search Engines

If you have a website with a host, it will usually be hosted within that companies main server, there, all relevant information is stored. Search engines serve the internet by helping users to track down and find information hidden away on other web sites, within their respective servers. Search engines execute the same tasks in principle and have their methods for providing the above service.

When a user searches for a specific piece of information, a user logs onto a computer, initiates an internet browser. i.e. Google, Safari, Mozilla, then enters a keyword(s) and tells the search engine to search the internet for information relevant to the keyword they have entered.

The search engine formulates an index and the location of the words it finds on that particular server. It allows the user to search for words and combinations of relevant words within that index.

Hopefully, now it has become apparent how important some metadata is in relation to search engines, regarding successful marketing and sales of your book.

DRM

Digital Rights Management in its simplest form is the restriction of content so that when an individual purchases media, for example, an eBook for their specified device, i.e. a Kindle, media cannot be shared on other devices, i.e. an iPad.

An aggregator may give you a choice, whether or not you want to apply DRM to your product. There are arguments for and against and plenty of articles to help you decide on the web.

BOOKBABY

An intuitive website and very user friendly. Everything is laid out at your disposal.

SETUP FEES

Free Package – $0, they retain 15% commission on net sales from online retailer partners.

You supply the ePub or .mobi file, they distribute the eBook globally.

Free Bookshop webpage that allows you to sell direct, you keep 85% net sales.

Standard Package - $99. They retain 15% commission on net sales from online retailer partners.

Includes ePub and .mobi file conversion, proof, worldwide distribution and additional services.

Free Bookshop webpage that allows you to sell direct, you keep 85% net sales.

Premium Package - $249. You keep 100% of net sales from online retailer partners.

Includes ePub and .mobi file conversion, proof, worldwide distribution, additional services, priority processing and delivery.

Free Bookshop webpage that allows you to sell direct, you keep 85% net sales.

For a detailed comparison list of services… Jump to BookBaby/Pricing

COMMISION

eBooks – Depends on which of the above service you chose.

Print on Demand - Available only to Author. Price calculated dependent on Quantity, Page Count, Binding, Cover type / finish, Paper stock and Add-ons. Don't forget additional delivery costs!

ISBN

19$. Sometimes Bookbaby offer deals!

SUPPORT

Yes

EBOOK CONVERSION

Yes, unless you opt for the Free Package.

TEMPLATES

Yes

BUILD COVER OPTION

eBook – No.

POD - No.

PROFESSIONAL SERVICES

Design, Editorial & Marketing all at an extra cost.

DISTRIBUTION

Amazon, Apple iBook store , Baker&Taylor, Ciando, Copia, e-sentral, flipkart.com, Gardners Books, Kobo, nook by Barnes & Noble, Oyster, Scribd.

FORMATS COMPATIBLE FOR FILE UPLOAD

Free Package - ePub and .mobi

Paid Packages - .doc .docx .rtf .txt .html .pdf .indd .pages .qxd

SALES REPORTS

Yes.

EXTRAS

Author website by hostbaby. Book Scanning at an extra cost and eBook press release.

Custom printed books. BookPromo.

Publishing Credits – Prepay for publishing multiple books at a discounted rate.

COMMENTS

Sign up, upload your manuscript, enter metadata, upload your cover (If required), write your synopsis, choose your book price and the services you require.

Custom printed books are pricey compared to Createspace. Print quality is reported to be of a high standard.

www.bookbaby.com

CREATESPACE
(AMAZON)

An intuitive website and very user friendly. Everything is laid out at your disposal.

SETUP FEES

No.

COMMISSION

Print on Demand - Determined using a royalty calculator.

FREE ISBN

Yes.

SUPPORT

Yes.

eBOOK CONVERSION

Not primarily. You can 'Publish on Kindle' option once you have completed the process.

PRINT ON DEMAND

You can print as little as one copy! A great solution without having to invest your money. Createspace take a commission off each sale made on Amazon. Most companies charge hundreds of pounds for this service. Self orders - You only pay for what you buy. No setup costs involved. One of the best rates out there. Do not forget additional delivery costs!

TEMPLATES

Yes. Manuscript and Book Cover templates are free to download.

BUILD COVER OPTION

Yes.

PROFESSIONAL SERVICES

Design, Editorial & Marketing in abundance, but at an extra cost.

DISTRIBUTION

Amazon.uk, Amazon.com.

FORMATS COMPATIBLE FOR FILE UPLOAD

Word, PDF.

SALES REPORTS

Free.

EXTRAS

Standard Distribution… Amazon.com, Amazon's European websites, You can link and sell via your website and also a link to your Createspace eStore.

Expanded Distribution… online retailers, bookstores, libraries, academic institutions, and distributors within the United States at an extra cost.

COMMENTS

Sign up, upload your manuscript, create or upload a cover, enter metadata, write your synopsis, choose your book price and the services you require.

If you wish to sell in the US you will require a US tax ID which you can apply for (See Links). Stick to the European service and you'll be fine.

It is reasonably straight forward to link both Kindle and print editions, even if the print edition is with another publisher, in the Amazon catalogue.

www.createspace.com

KDP
(KINDLE DIRECT PUBLISHING – AMAZON)

An intuitive website and very user friendly. Everything is laid out at your disposal.

SETUP FEES

No.

COMMISSION

35% & 70% royalty program.

FREE ISBN

Yes.

SUPPORT

Yes.

eBOOK CONVERSION

Yes.

PRINT ON DEMAND

No. See Createspace.

TEMPLATES

Manuscript and Book Cover are free to download.

BUILD COVER OPTION

No.

PROFESSIONAL SERVICES

Conversion, Design, Editorial & Marketing in abundance, but at an extra cost.

DISTRIBUTION

Amazon.uk, Amazon.com.

FORMATS COMPATIBLE FOR FILE UPLOAD

.doc .docx .zip .htm .html .mobi .epub .rtf /txt .pdf

SALES REPORTS

Free.

EXTRAS

Publishing territories – select Worldwide rights or Individual Territories. Amazon.com, Amazon's European websites.

You can link and sell via your website and also link to your Createspace eStore.

Publish in multiple languages.

COMMENTS

Sign up, enter title information, upload your manuscript, cover, add synopsis, confirm publishing rights, enter book price and royalty information and select any additional services you require then submit for publishing.

It is reasonably straight forward to link both Kindle and print editions, even if the print edition is with another publisher, in the Amazon catalogue.

https://kdp.amazon.com

LULU

An intuitive, eye pleasing website, user friendly with lots of options.

SETUP FEES

Do-it-Yourself – £0. ePub conversion tool.

Upload your file, create a cover, describe your book, pick a price & promote your book.

The Assistant - £69. All of the above, handling and distribution.

The Insider - £99. All of the above, helix review.

The Amplifier – £149. All of the above, free 6x9 perfect bound paperback copy of your book (black and white interior), formatting and a clean Lulu galley cover design for the print version of the book.

Go Pro – One on one assistance, custom cover design, interior design and layout. POA.

To see a detailed comparison list of services…

http://www.lulu.com/publish/ebooks/

COMMISION

eBooks - You receive 90% of the revenue from the sales of your book.

Print on Demand – Determined using a royalty calculator.

FREE ISBN

Yes.

SUPPORT

Yes.

eBOOK CONVERSION

Yes.

PRINT ON DEMAND

An abundance of options at varying rates. Free distribution to Amazon, Barnes & Noble, Ingram Catalogue. Higher revenue is earned selling direct via Lulu platform.

TEMPLATES

Yes.

BUILD COVER OPTION

Yes.

PROFESSIONAL SERVICES

Design, Editorial & Marketing all at an extra cost.

DISTRIBUTION

eBook – Amazon, iBook store, Kobo, Nook by Barnes & Noble & Lulu.com

Print – Amazon, Barnes & Noble, Ingram.

FORMATS COMPATIBLE FOR FILE UPLOAD

Lulu Marketplace - .docx, .epub .jpg .pdf .png .rtf

Retail Channels - .epub

SALES REPORTS

Included.

EXTRAS

Lulu have a decent online store and good author packages.

COMMENTS

Sign up, upload your manuscript, create or upload your cover, write your synopsis, choose your book price and the services you require.

If choosing the Do-It-Yourself option, then download

the eBook Creator Guide.

www.lulu.com

NOOK PRESS
(BARNES AND NOBLE)

Designed to enable the Self-publisher to do exactly just that. Simple, straight forward and user friendly.

SETUP FEES

No.

COMMISSION

40% & 65%.

FREE ISBN

No. Nook assign a unique identifier (nook's own internal number for their system) called the 'BN ID'. You can assign an ISBN if you already have one.

SUPPORT

Yes.

EBOOK CONVERSION

Nook use an internal 'Manuscript Editor' that allows you to 'Start a new Project' or 'Upload' a file.

PRINT ON DEMAND

No.

TEMPLATES

No. Not required if you use Nook's 'Manuscript Editor'.

BUILD COVER OPTION

No.

PROFESSIONAL SERVICES

Nook seem to have focused solely on self-publishing. There seem to be no paid services available.

DISTRIBUTION

Barnes & Noble.

FORMATS COMPATIBLE FOR FILE UPLOAD

.doc .docx .epub .html .rtf .txt

SALES REPORTS

Yes.

EXTRAS

e-Gifting. Collaboration - You can invite others to collaborate on your manuscript or collaborate on theirs.

COMMENTS

A simple, friendly user interface with lots of useful guides to help you along.

Limited distribution network, though Barnes and Noble hold a respectable position within the marketplace.

www.nookpress.com

SMASHWORDS

An intuitive, eye pleasing website, user friendly with lots of options.

SETUP FEES

No.

COMMISION

eBooks - 60% list price from major ebook distributors & 85% net from Smashwords.com

FREE ISBN

Yes.

SUPPORT

Yes.

EBOOK CONVERSION

Yes. Multiple formats.

PRINT ON DEMAND

No.

TEMPLATES

No. You can download their 'Style Guide'.

BUILD COVER OPTION

Yes

PROFESSIONAL SERVICES

Design, Editorial & Marketing all at an extra cost.

DISTRIBUTION

Aldiko, axis360, blio, flipkart, iBook store, Barnes & Noble, fnac, Kobo, OverDrive, Oyster, Page Foundry, Scribd, Smashwords Store, 'txtr, WHSmith.

FORMATS COMPATIBLE FOR FILE UPLOAD

.doc ePub and also professionally designed .epub files.

SALES REPORTS

Yes.

EXTRAS

Free unlimited anytime-updates of metadata. Free

exclusive marketing and selling tools.

COMMENTS

Sign up, upload your manuscript, create your cover (If required), write your synopsis, choose your book price and the services you require.

www.smashwords.com

GOODREADS

The 'Goodreads Author Program' is a free service that serves the needs of authors wanting to promote their titles and reach a target audience. Whether you have already published or are about to self-publish, this is worth considering. Goodreads recommend that you first have your title with an aggregator / distributor before registering and adding to their site.

www.goodreads.com/author/program

HINDSIGHT

So now you have the facts. You have all the relevant information to get you started, and I have listed, what I deem the six best aggregators for your consideration.

How I went about it...

Having my polished manuscript, synopsis and artwork at the ready, I downloaded a template from Amazon's 'Createspace' and then copied and pasted my manuscript onto the template. It proved a little fiddly and time-consuming. As mentioned earlier, everything was misaligned, words were missing and, as a result, I had to recheck the whole document to pacify my paranoia. It can be most frustrating, the clock is ticking, and you want to crack on, but remember to take your time and check it over thoroughly when done. Imagine, submitting and publishing your work only to receive negative reviews pointing out basic grammatical mistakes. It does not serve your reputation and would be detrimental to the sales of your book. Also, if you did employ the services of an editor, it would reflect poorly on your editor and undo all their good work.

After I had long tormented over whom to publish with I decided to publish my eBook with BookBaby. They had a decent amount of distributors attached to their portfolio and at the time they offered a free ISBN with their basic package. I did not require any additional services and was all set to go. I signed up, filled in my details, uploaded my files, manuscript and artwork, added my synopsis, entered the metadata and keywords and decided on a price. Note, the price you set isn't always the price your distributors go with.

Bookbaby allows you to select from a number of distribution partners within their portfolio and has since expanded. Once the account is active, you can log in and monitor status reports as and when each party has received your book. I found the process to be simple and efficient.

The first few months, sales exceed my expectation; I had climbed to number 80 in the iTunes book chart. They tapered off as following months passed. Inevitable I suppose as more and more self-publishers flooded the market, nudging my book into obscurity. Fortunately, I had managed to recoup my $99 sign-up fee within the first month, so the rest was profit.

I began to assess and wonder how I could have done better. I regularly browsed the rankings table on both Amazon and iTunes and soon it became all so apparent. The big named authors, yes those backed by the publishing giants we all resent, but want to share a bed with, demanded top dollar and held their spots well, but they were not alone. Others, names I had never heard of held their heads high and made their presence known amongst the ranks. I eyed their covers, read their synopsis, mused over their titles… they were good, but what had my attention was their price.

I had had my shot and had let it slip by. I knew I had out priced myself and missed the opportunity to climb the rankings and get noticed. Lesson learned. I cannot stress enough, know your aggregator and the services that they offer. Ask yourself what services do they offer you the others cannot. Do you really need all the services they offer? Do not buy into all the hype.

Bookbaby has amassed a vast distribution network. It was the deciding factor when considering which aggregator to pledge my allegiance. Only two have served my purpose and generated sales of my book, Amazon, whom I consider the biggest mover and shaker in this arena and of course iTunes. It is not that straightforward publishing directly with iTunes as you have to go through the rigmarole of acquiring a US tax ID.

I decided on BookBaby's upfront promotional fee of $99 in which I also got a free ISBN (now the Standard Package), though reduced, it was still an initial outlay, $99 that I had to recoup. It is worth noting, Smashwords and Lulu, also have iTunes in their portfolio, and charge nothing upfront, supply a free ISBN and take their cut off the back of the sale. If you sell a vast amount of books, doubtful in most cases, then it possibly might work in your favour going with BookBaby.

KDP assigns a free ISBN and obviously distribute directly via Amazon as they are part of the Amazon group, so it is in-house. I had considered KDP before deciding to go with BookBaby, but their service seemed limited. It is not. They have a vast distribution network and even without, command a huge percentage of the market being part of Amazon. It was not until I decided to explore P.O.D with Amazon's 'Createspace' that I truly appreciated their presence.

If you are considering P.O.D. and wish to submit a manuscript with Creatspace, it is a simple process. Once you have signed up, you will discover everything neatly laid out and easy to follow. The customer service team are helpful and responsive. Their user account offers many options and tools that you can utilize as and when you are ready to do so.

Within a week, I had uploaded my manuscript, and it was available on the Amazon website featured alongside my eBook. If you wish to order copies, you can order as many as you want at a discounted rate, and they will arrive by post within a few weeks. But remember the advice I gave earlier, operate as a business, don't spend your money unless you have people committed to orders (unless ordering for gifts), we are talking business here.

Once you have uploaded your manuscript with Createspace and gone through all the formalities, you can then publish your work as an eBook simply by selecting 'Publish on Kindle.' It will direct you to a page that requests you sign in with your Amazon account. As above, everything is set before you in neat, easy to follow instructions. Enter your details, metadata, tick a few boxes, upload your cover and manuscript and before you know it, you've not only got your book as POD, but also as an eBook. Obviously Amazon takes their cut, but you have done away with the middleman. It is a one-stop solution to all your self-publishing needs.

CONCLUSION

All of the aggregators I have mentioned offer an excellent service. However, for future projects, I have decided to concentrate on Amazon's 'Createspace.' The lure of having a huge network of distributors at my feet with BookBaby did not fulfill my expectations, admittedly, marketing on my part could have been better. Don't think for one-minute that an aggregator is going to market your book. Not unless you are going to pay them.

All sales for my title came via Amazon and iTunes, I have sold one title via Barnes and Noble. Dealing direct means, I do not have to pay the aggregator a percentage or an upfront fee and maintenance fee for every year thereafter. If I decide to target the iTunes market, then I can always use Smashwords or Lulu who as explained earlier take a percentage off the back end. I can live with that, still, I have not parted with my money. And of course, Nook Press, who distributes under Barnes and Noble, who also take their money off the back end, so once Createspace have allocated you a free ISBN, you can publish via them too. With that in mind, remember, your requirements may differ from mine. Maybe you do not have the time to go about it in that manner, you don't mind investing a little capital, and want to hand your work off so you can begin another project. If so, then BookBaby has it all covered and is an excellent option.

Most of the aggregators offer an expanded distribution network for bookstores, online retailers, libraries and academic institutions. Although it sounds grand, in short, they send your book data to major bibliographical databases such as 'Nielson and Bowker' and 'Gardners,' who then order and stock your title according to demand from retail outlets at the request of the customer. I am yet to benefit from this. Remember, your customers have to be aware of your book, you have to drive demand and that requires a well thought out marketing strategy.

Marketing was certainly my Achilles heel. I simply don't have the time. I want to concentrate on writing my next project; that is what I do, write. You need to think this one out. Have a plan. Blog, utilise social networking sites to drive customers to your product, after all, they are free. If you feel compelled to up the ante publicising your book, keep it to a minimum, print business cards with links directing people to the websites advertising and hosting your book, hand them out, leave them around in random places, but be subtle and considerate. Most Aggregators blog and provide an abundance of self-help guides. It serves them to do so, maybe they will serve you too.

Writing a book to then self-publish doesn't have to be all about business, Sure, I got serious writing my first book. I wanted it to be a success (my interpretation of success will probably differ to yours), and if I am honest it wasn't all that much fun, challenging actually. Probably because self-publishing became all about business. I think it is important to realise your expectations. Why do you want to self-publish? Chances are you will not make any money.

If you want to publish or print your book so you can give it as a gift or simply have it as a keepsake, do not spend a penny. Use 'Grammarly' as your editor, ask an artistic friend to do your cover or have a go yourself and use Amazon (Createspace / KDP) to be your aggregator. That is exactly what I have done for this project for the purpose of demonstrating 'Pub It Yourself'.

Grammarly, is a website, not a person that you sign up to for a nominal fee. It is far cheaper than hiring an editor, but has its limitations. For starters, this is a factual piece I have written, not fiction. Plot, story, character, irony, humour, emotion, etc. would be best-left to a human. However, if you are strong in all of the above and only require an automated proofreader and grammar coach, then maybe it's all you need to get the job done?

PITCH IN

I hope this book serves you to accomplish all your writing goals. Please remember I am no expert, far from it. But we can share what we know and educate each other.

Visit my website 'PUB IT' page for an abundance of writing, self-publishing guides and utilities.

www.savvy-selfpublishing.com

Self-publishing can be a daunting prospect. Please share this site with others and also be generous with the knowledge you have attained. If you have any useful hints, tips, trick or links then please PITCH IN here...

www.savvy-selfpublishing.com/pitch-in/

I wish you well.

ABOUT THE AUTHOR

Zachary Black self-published his first title, 'Body Bags and Shallow Graves' in 2010. He has since written several unsolicited scripts and is currently writing the second draft of his next title.